"HELLO READING books are a perfect introduction to reading. Brief sentences full of word repetition and full-color pictures stress visual clues to help a child take the first important steps toward reading. Mastering these story books will build children's reading confidence and give them the enthusiasm to stand on their own in the world of words."

—Bee Cullinan
Past President of the International Reading Association, Professor in New York University's Early Childhood and Elementary Education Program

"Readers aren't born, they're made. Desire is planted—planted by parents who work at it."

—Jim Trelease
author of *The Read Aloud Handbook*

"When I was a classroom reading teacher, I recognized the importance of good stories in making children understand that reading is more than just recognizing words. I saw that children who have ready access to story books get excited about reading. They also make noticeably greater gains in reading comprehension. The development of the HELLO READING stories grows out of this experience."

—Harriet Ziefert
M.A.T., New York University School of Education
Author, Language Arts Module,
Scholastic Early Childhood Program

For Lynn Seiffer

PUFFIN BOOKS
Published by the Penguin Group
27 Wrights Lane, London W8 5TZ, England
Viking Penguin Inc., 40 West 23rd Street, New York, New York 10010, USA
Penguin Books Australia Ltd, Ringwood, Victoria, Australia
Penguin Books Canada Ltd, 2801 John Street, Markham, Ontario, Canada L3R 1B4
Penguin Books (NZ) Ltd, 182–190 Wairau Road, Auckland 10, New Zealand

Penguin Books Ltd, Registered Offices: Harmondsworth, Middlesex, England

First published in the USA in Puffin Books 1990
This edition published in Great Britain 1990
10 9 8 7 6 5 4 3 2 1
Text copyright © Harriet Ziefert, 1990
Illustrations copyright © Mary Morgan, 1990
All rights reserved

Text anglicized by Jill Bennett

Printed in Singapore for Harriet Ziefert, Inc.

Except in the United States of America,
this book is sold subject to the condition that
it shall not, by way of trade or otherwise,
be lent, re-sold, hired out, or otherwise circulated
without the publisher's prior consent in any form of
binding or cover other than that in which it is
published and without a similar condition
including this condition being imposed
on the subsequent purchaser

Let's Swap

**Harriet Ziefert
Pictures by Mary Morgan**

PUFFIN BOOKS

"Have a nice picnic!"
said Mum.

Meg, Sam and Jo
took their lunch bags.

They went to the park.
Their cat went too.

"I've got a cucumber and some grapes," said Meg.
"Sam, what have you got?"

"A banana,"
said Sam.
"And I'm sick of bananas."

"I like bananas," said Meg.
"Let's swap."

Sam gave Meg the banana.
Meg gave Sam the cucumber.

"What have you got?"
Meg asked Jo.

"A peanut butter sandwich," said Jo.
"I'm sick of peanut butter!"

"I like peanut butter," said Meg.
"Let's swap."

Jo gave Meg the sandwich.
Meg gave Jo the grapes.

"What have you got?"
Jo asked Meg.

"I have a banana and
a peanut butter sandwich,"
said Meg.

"But you've got *two* things!" said Sam and Jo together. "It's not fair!"

"I'll be fair!" said Meg.
"I'll share!"

Meg shared the banana.
Meg shared the sandwich.

"Now you've got more than me!"
Meg said to Sam and Jo.
"You've got *three* things each!"

Sam ate the cucumber
and the peanut butter sandwich—
but *not* the banana!

"Remember," he said,
"I'm sick of bananas!"

Jo ate the grapes
and the banana—
but *not* the peanut butter
sandwich.

"Remember," she said,
"I'm sick of peanut butter!"

Meg put her banana on top
of the peanut butter.
She ate it all up.
"Yummy!" she said.

"Yuck!" said Sam.
"Yuck!" said Jo.

"You wanted *my* food," said Meg.
"Now eat it all up!"

"No," said Sam.
"I won't eat the banana!"

"No," said Jo.
"I won't eat peanut butter."

"Now listen to me," said Meg.

"Sam, swap with Jo.
Jo, swap with Sam."

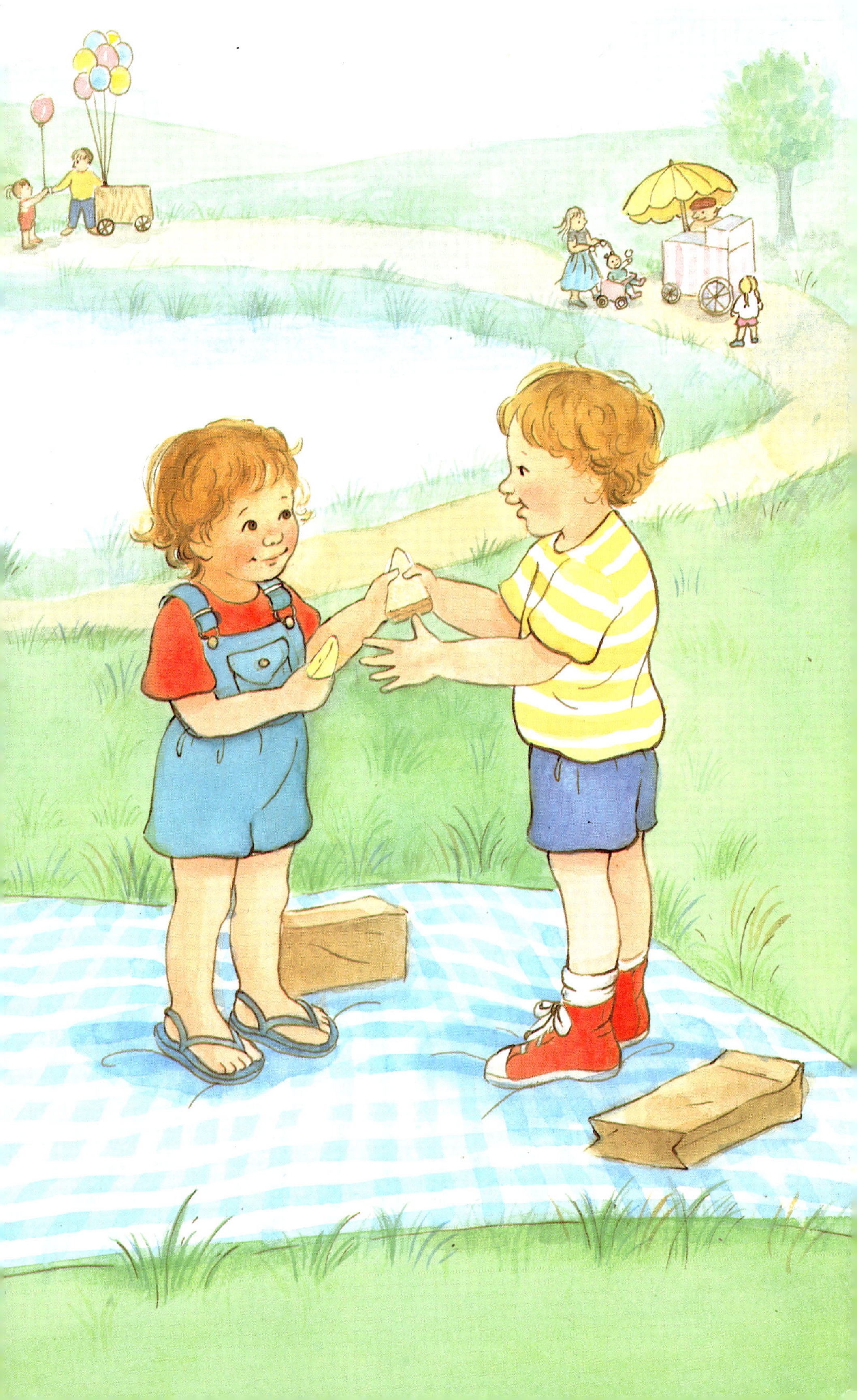

"Bossyboots!" said Sam to Meg.
But he ate the sandwich.

"Bossyboots," said Jo to Meg.
But she ate the banana.

"Now let's play softball," said Meg.

"I can't play," said Sam.
"My glove is too small."

"And I can't play," said Jo.
"My glove is too big."

Sam looked at Jo.
Jo looked at Sam.

"Let's swap!" said Sam.

"Right, let's play!" said Meg.